WORKBOOK

Living in the Victory of JESUS!

A. OKECHUKWU OGBONNAYA, PH.D.

Printed in the USA.

All proper names mentioned in this publication are fictional unless otherwise indicated.

Unless otherwise noted, all Scripture is taken from the KJV.

Item #: 6-08550
ISBN-13: 978-1-60352-091-1
ISBN-10: 1-60352-091-0

Publisher: UMI (Urban Ministries, Inc.), Chicago, IL 60643

To place an order: Call us at 1-800-860-8642 or visit our website at www.urbanministries.com.

TABLE OF CONTENTS

ANNOUNCING VICTORY

BASED ON MATTHEW 1:18–25

KEY VERSE: *"But while he thought on these things, behold, the angel of the LORD appeared unto him in a dream, saying, Joseph, thou son of David, fear not to take unto thee Mary thy wife: for that which is conceived in her is of the Holy Ghost"* (Matthew 1:20).

LESSON FOCUS

Jesus' birth ushered in several victories, all of which are available to believers today. Because of Jesus' sacrifice, we can be victors over sin. Our victory over sin reconciles us to God, and we can live victorious and abundant lives because God is with us. Because we have the victory, fear can be dispelled and we have the power and freedom to live as God has commissioned each of us. Are you allowing Jesus to help you live victoriously?

DO YOU KNOW...?

To prepare for this lesson, study the following words and definitions (all are taken from Chapter 1—"Announcing Victory").

betrothal—dowry (goods/money) exchanged for the bride

Christ—the Anointed One, the Messiah

Messiah—Anointed One

patriarchal—male-dominated

INTRODUCTION (REAL LIFE) DISCUSSION QUESTIONS

After reading the Introduction (Real Life) section, answer the following questions.

1. Explain your understanding of a "sin nature."

____

____

____

2. Why is Jesus the Champion, or Victor, over sin?

____

3. Name three persons in your life who have been champions for you. What made them champions, or victors?

4. If Jesus is your Champion, or Victor, how do you share His victory in your life with others?

5. Why do you think someone struggling with an addiction finds it hard to give his/her addiction over to the Lord? What are the issues in your life that you are unable to turn over to the Lord and why?

A WORD FROM THE LORD

SCRIPTURE SEARCH

Read Matthew 1:18–25, and then use the following questions to review the facts from this Scripture passage.

Matthew lists four women in Jesus' family line, an uncommon practice among the male-dominated society. Use a concordance to find the four women mentioned in the genealogy; use the Scripture to describe the women. What lessons can we learn about God's kingdom through their stories?

a. Tamar (Genesis 38:1–30)

b. Rahab (Joshua 2:1–24; 6:24–25)

c. Ruth (Ruth 1–4)

d. Bathsheba, Uriah's wife (2 Samuel 11:1–27; 12:24–25)

Victory over Biology

Jesus' birth points to His divinity and His humanity. While He entered the world as a human born to a woman, His birth was no ordinary birth. He was conceived by the Holy Spirit. Use the Scriptures listed below to discuss Jesus' two natures and how they affect us.

a. Human Nature (Hebrews 2:14–18; Romans 8:3–4)

b. Divine Nature (John 1:1–5, 10–13)

Victory in His Name

1. Emmanuel means "God with us." Make up an acrostic for the name *Emmanuel* to describe what "God with us" means to you. Find a Scripture to support each description.

E__________ Scripture __________

M__________ Scripture __________

M__________ Scripture __________

A__________ Scripture __________

N__________ Scripture __________

U__________ Scripture __________

E__________ Scripture __________

L__________ Scripture __________

2. Jesus means "the Lord Saves." Make up an acrostic for the name *Jesus* to describe what "the Lord Saves" means to you. Find a Scripture to support each description.

J________________________ Scripture ________________________

E________________________ Scripture ________________________

S________________________ Scripture ________________________

U________________________ Scripture ________________________

S________________________ Scripture ________________________

Victory over Anxiety

The angel in today's lesson helped Joseph alleviate his anxiety over Mary's pregnancy. Review how God has relieved anxiety in others.

a. Elijah (1 Kings 19:9–18)

____

____

____

b. Gideon (Judges 6:11–24)

____

____

____

c. Hannah (1 Samuel 1:10–20)

____

____

____

d. the disciples (Luke 8:22–25)

____

____

____

MAKING THE DIFFERENCE (COMMUNITY)

After reading the Making the Difference (Community) section, answer the following questions.

1. Joseph was both religious and obedient. How can a church benefit from members who display both characteristics? How is a church affected when its members are more religious than obedient?

2. What are some things churches can do to promote obedience to God among members?

3. List some of the various ministries in your church. How are they motivated by love and obedience? How would emphasizing their motives benefit members?

LIVING IN VICTORY (PERSONAL)

After reading the Living in Victory (Personal) section, answer the following questions.

1. List the persons who you consider your best friends and/or protectors? How is your relationship with them compared to your relationship with Jesus?

2. What is your relationship with God, and does it need to change or grow? If yes, how does it need to change or grow?

3. Read 1 Corinthians 10:13. Consider how you can adjust your perspective according to the Word of God, when in the midst of rough times and have a new perspective on who Jesus is to you?

PRAYER FORUM

Write a prayer or words of inspiration related to the chapter's theme.

FROM DEFEAT TO VICTORY

BASED ON LUKE 15:11–24

KEY VERSE: *"For this my son was dead, and is alive again; he was lost, and is found. And they began to be merry"* (Luke 15:24).

LESSON FOCUS

The story of the Prodigal Son reminds us of God's desire for the lost to be found and for the broken to be made whole. Because of God's grace and love, we can run into our Lord's open arms and receive the victory over all defeat. In God's arms, we can bring our hopelessness and exchange it for a bright new hope; we can bring our insecurities and insufficiencies, and leave with the blessed assurance that God will take care of all our needs. Yes, when we run back to our Father, we can experience the Master stroke of divine mercy.

DO YOU KNOW. . . ?

To prepare for this lesson, study the following words and definitions (all are taken from Chapter 2—"From Defeat to Victory").

dietary laws—the directions given by God regarding which foods could be eaten by the Jews

fatted calf—the choicest animal

Gentiles—non-Jewish people or tribes

inheritance—goods given to an heir or beneficiary after the death of the initial owner

prodigal—irresponsibly wasteful or careless

INTRODUCTION (REAL LIFE) DISCUSSION QUESTIONS

After reading the Introduction (Real Life) section, answer the following questions.

1. The opening statement of Chapter 2 says: "Selfishness tends to breed impatience." Explain whether or not you agree with that statement and share examples to support your opinion.

____

____

____

2. "Pride goeth before destruction, and an haughty spirit before a fall" (Proverbs 16:18). Share examples from modern media of this proverb and be prepared to discuss whether this same principle applies to the lives of those who have accepted Christ and those who have not.

3. Think of a modern-day situation that fits the circumstances that prompted Jesus to tell the story of the Prodigal Son: religious people like the Pharisees and scribes murmuring about sinners.

A WORD FROM THE LORD

SCRIPTURE SEARCH

Read Luke 15:11–24, and then use the following questions to review the facts from this Scripture passage.

1. Read Luke 15:1–10. Why were the Pharisees and scribes critical of Jesus?

2. How does the parable address the Pharisees' and scribes' complaint about Jesus?

3. Why do you think the Prodigal Son wanted his inheritance early (Luke 15:12)?

4. What happened when the son moved away (v. 13)?

5. What made the son decide to return home (v. 17)?

6. How did the father react when his son returned (vv. 22–24)?

____

____

Where Selfish Desires Lead

The Prodigal Son was motivated by selfish desires to ask for his inheritance before his father died. Look up the following Scriptures and fill in the blanks to complete the Scripture. Be prepared to discuss what they have in common.

1. "But every man is ___________, when he is drawn away of his own _______, and __________. Then when lust hath conceived, it bringeth forth _______: and _______, when it is finished, bringeth forth _______" (James 1:14-15).

2. "Let nothing be done through _______ or ___________; but in ___________ of mind let each esteem other better than themselves. Look not every man on his ________ things, but every man also on the things of __________. Let this _______ be in you, which was also in ________ _________" (Philippians 2:3–5).

3. "And the LORD said unto Cain, Why art thou __________? and why is thy countenance fallen? If thou doest well, shalt thou not be accepted? and if thou doest not well, _______ lieth at the door. And unto thee shall be his _________, and thou shalt rule over him" (Genesis 4:6–7).

4. "Let us not be ___________ of ______ _________, provoking one another, ____________ one another" (Galatians 5:26).

Seeking Satisfaction

The Prodigal Son went off to find happiness and satisfaction, which are arguably what most people are searching for. Christians should know that all we're searching for can be found in accepting Christ and knowing God. Write how each Scripture can be explained and used to help those who are seeking satisfaction in their search.

1. "Come unto me, all ye that labour and are heavy laden, and I will give you rest. Take my yoke upon you, and learn of me; for I am meek and lowly in heart: and ye shall find rest unto your souls" (Matthew 11:28).

____

____

____

____

2. "Ask, and it shall be given you; seek, and ye shall find; knock, and it shall be opened unto you: For every one that asketh receiveth; and he that seeketh findeth; and to him that knocketh it shall be opened" (Matthew 7:7–8).

____

____

____

3. "The LORD is my light and my salvation; whom shall I fear? the LORD is the strength of my life; of whom shall I be afraid?" (Psalm 27:1).

____

____

____

____

4. "I will lift up mine eyes unto the hills, from whence cometh my help. My help cometh from the LORD, which made heaven and earth" (Psalm 121:1–2).

____

____

____

____

5. "And we know that all things work together for good to them that love God, to them who are the called according to his purpose" (Romans 8:28).

____

____

____

____

6. "But my God shall supply all you need according to his riches in glory by Christ Jesus" (Philippians 4:19).

____

____

____

____

7. "Be careful for nothing; but in every thing by prayer and supplication with thanksgiving let your requests be made known unto God. And the peace of God, which passeth all understanding, shall keep your hearts and minds through Christ Jesus" (Philippians 4:6–7).

____

____

____

____

8. "Delight thyself also in the LORD: and he shall give thee the desires of thine heart" (Psalm 37:4).

____

Hitting Rock Bottom

Reread Luke 15:11–24. List several adjectives to describe how the Prodigal Son must have been feeling in each scene of his life.

1. When he asked for his inheritance (Luke 15:12)

2. When he received his inheritance and moved away (v. 13)

3. When all of his money was gone and he was hungry (vv. 14–16)

4. When he decided he'd go home and ask for a position as a servant (vv. 17–19)

Review the adjectives. Circle the adjectives that describe something you or someone you know has experienced. How could this story be used to help that person or yourself? (Discuss the choices.)

MAKING THE DIFFERENCE (COMMUNITY)

After reading the Making the Difference (Community) section, answer the following questions.

1. What are some positive steps that your congregation can take to help welcome the lost into the fold?

2. What protective measures can be taken, by the church and fellow Christians, to provide an environment to help strengthen a person so that he or she will not readily or hastily fall back into old patterns of sinful behavior?

3. How can you and fellow members sensitize yourselves so that you do not become angry or resentful of those who have strayed from God yet returned?

4. Consider making a list comparing the benefits of showing forgiveness and compassion to others versus acting toward others with judgment and resentment. Which set of behaviors will yield the greatest results for God's kingdom? Discuss.

LIVING IN VICTORY (PERSONAL)

After reading the Living in Victory (Personal) section, answer the following questions.

1. Which character do you relate to the most: the Prodigal Son, the father, or the Pharisees and scribes? Explain your answer.

2. How can today's Scripture lesson help you view others as God views us?

3. Sometimes people must endure hard experiences in order to recognize the blessings that have always been available to them. Write some of your blessings and thank God for them more frequently.

PRAYER FORUM

Write a prayer or words of inspiration thanking God for a victory He has placed or is placing in your life or the life of someone for whom you have concern.

VICTORY OVER GRIEF

BASED ON MARK 5:1–19, 21–24, 35–43

KEY VERSE: *"And always, night and day, he was in the mountains, and in the tombs, crying, and cutting himself with stones"* (Mark 5:5).

LESSON FOCUS

The sense of loss is deeply felt when a loved one is lost or missed. Loss changes our posture. It has a direct impact upon our lives. Loss unnerves us and frees us to become vulnerable. Death, however, is not the only loss that we encounter in our earthly journey. There are other losses of small and great proportion.

In all our losses, these questions must be asked: How can we begin anew? How can we rise from the ashes? Is it possible to live again—to live anew? The answer is to turn to the One with whom we need a deeper connection—the One called a "man of sorrow acquainted with grief."

DO YOU KNOW. . . ?

To prepare for this lesson, study the following words and definitions (all are taken from Chapter 3—"Victory over Grief").

antithetical—opposing, negating, adverse, hostile

faith—assurance, confidence, conviction, trust

grief—anguish, heartache, misery, pain, sorrow

grieve—be distressed, feel sad, lament, to mourn

loss—bereavement, death, deficit, demise, injury, hurt

INTRODUCTION (REAL LIFE) DISCUSSION QUESTIONS

After reading the Introduction (Real Life) section, answer the following questions.

1. How did the author and his family grieve in the loss of their loved ones?

a. ______________________________

b. ______________________________

c. ______________________________

d. ______________________________

e. ______________________________

f. ______________________________

2. Why did the author grieve over his son?

____

____

3. Name four ways that loss affects our general experience as human beings.

a. ______________________________

b. ______________________________

c. ______________________________

d. ______________________________

4. Explain how some people deny the pain of loss.

____

____

5. The denial of loss is ______________ to faith. Explain what this statement means.

____

____

____

____

6. Share a personal experience of loss or grief and how God brought you through.

____

____

____

A WORD FROM THE LORD

SCRIPTURE SEARCH

Read Mark 5:1–19, 21–24, 35–43, and then use the following questions to review the facts from this Scripture passage.

1. What was the problem that caused Jairus to seek out Jesus and beg for His help (Mark 5:23)?

2. On the way to Jairus's house, Jesus was delayed by a woman with an issue of blood. What message did Jairus receive from home during this delay (v. 35)?

3. When Jesus arrived at Jairus's house, there was a great crowd. What was the crowd doing (v. 38)?

4. Who were the five people who entered the child's room with Jesus (v. 40)?

5. Jesus spoke to the dead girl, and she arose and walked around. What effect did this have on those in the room with Jesus (v. 42)?

6. Look up and define the words *dead* and *asleep*. Then discuss in what sense a believer sleeps rather than dies.

MAKING THE DIFFERENCE (COMMUNITY)

After reading the Making the Difference (Community) section, answer the following questions.

1. The life expectancy of African American males has declined due to gang violence. Can faith in Christ make a difference? If so, whose responsibility is it to take the Gospel message to them? Explain.

2. What is the church's responsibility toward its members who are grieving or expressing a loss? Explain.

LIVING IN VICTORY (PERSONAL)

After reading the Living in Victory (Personal) section, answer the following questions.

1. Faith is the remedy for fear. When facing a crisis, how should you use your faith in Christ to overcome fear?

2. Think of a situation that is causing you grief. How have you been handling it? Has the grief caused you to misplace your trust? What can you do to change that?

3. Explain how not dealing with a loss can lead one to self-destructive behaviors. What can you do to safeguard yourself from such an occurrence?

PRAYER FORUM

Write a prayer or words of inspiration thanking God for being a very present help in your times of grief and loss.

THE POWER OF JESUS: VICTORY OVER SIN AND SICKNESS

BASED ON MARK 2:3–12

KEY VERSES: *"But that ye may know that the Son of man hath power on earth to forgive sins, (he saith to the sick of the palsy,) I say unto thee, Arise, and take up thy bed, and go thy way into thine house"* (Mark 2:10–11).

LESSON FOCUS

Because of the fall of Adam and Eve in the Garden of Eden (Genesis 3), sin came upon all humanity. The fact that they questioned God's goodness and disobeyed Him when He told them not to eat from the Tree of Knowledge of Good and Evil, sin was imputed to us all. Now we are born in sin. It took Jesus Christ, God's one and only Son, to come to Earth to pay our sin penalty. Then and only then were we able to restore our broken relationship with a Holy (set apart from sin) God. Because of what Jesus did on Calvary, we can have victory over sin and sickness.

DO YOU KNOW. . . ?

To prepare for this lesson, study the following words and definitions (all are taken from Chapter 4—"The Power of Jesus: Victory over Sin and Sickness").

affirmation—confirmation, verification

blasphemy—profanity, sacrilege

divine authority—power and abilities that come from God

faith—confidence, trust, reliance

forgive—to release a person from the harm that he/she has done to you; to obey God's command to release the person from the infraction

INTRODUCTION (REAL LIFE) DISCUSSION QUESTIONS

After reading the Introduction (Real Life) section, answer the following questions.

1. Share how you felt once you knew that God had forgiven you of your sins (saved you). If you are not saved, share how you felt upon being forgiven by a friend or loved one for causing them great pain.

2. Share how you felt upon being healed of a sickness.

A WORD FROM THE LORD

SCRIPTURE SEARCH

Read Mark 2:3–12, and then use the following questions to review the facts from this Scripture passage.

1. When word of Jesus' return to Capernaum got out, how did the people react (Mark 2:3)?

2. When the men carrying the paralyzed man on a stretcher arrived at the house where Jesus was, their way was blocked by a huge crowd. How did they finally get the paralytic to Jesus (v. 4)?

3. How did the religious leaders react when Jesus told the man His sins were forgiven (v. 7)?

4. What two emotions did Jesus experience when He saw the callousness of the religious leaders' hearts (v. 5)?

5. The healing of the man in today's lesson affirmed Christ and glorified God. Besides divine healing, discuss some ways that our infirmities may be used to bring glory and honor to God.

6. Jesus became angry with the Pharisees' attitude toward the afflicted man. He responded to the situation by healing the man of his affliction. Discuss what lesson about anger believers can learn from this episode.

7. Each of the following Scriptures demonstrates the healing power of Jesus. For each one, name the ailment, and tell whether Jesus healed the physical, spiritual, or both. Then name the ailment.

a. Matthew 4:23–24

b. Matthew 9:2

c. Luke 8:43–44

d. Mark 2:3–5, 11–12

e. Luke 14:3–4

f. Luke 23:40–43

8. Read Psalm 103:3 and James 5:15. Discuss what our attitude should be concerning healing and forgiveness.

Power of Sin Broken

If you have Jesus, the power of sin in your life is broken. Victory over sin will not keep you from falling, but it gives you the power to start anew. You see, true victory leads to freedom.

1. In Galatians 5:13 (NIV), we are told that we were "called to be free." But that freedom does not come without warning. What is the warning mentioned?

2. The following verses, from Galatians 5, name different acts of our sinful nature. Name some of the acts mentioned and modern-day examples of each.

a. verse 19

b. verse 20

c. verse 21

d. Modern-day examples

3. We are also told in Galatians 5:13 (NIV) to "serve one another in love." Explain how our victory over sin should allow us to serve others in love.

Victory through Networking

As illustrated in Mark 2:3–12, a network of faith is necessary in a Christian's track toward victory. In fact, Jesus encourages it. Note His statement: "Where two or three are gathered together in my name, there am I in the midst of them."

1. Read the following Scriptures and discuss how each speaks on our responsibility as part of a network of faith.

a. 1 Corinthians 12:25–27

b. Romans 13:8

c. Ephesians 4:32

2. Ephesians 4:4 tells us we were called to one—one body, one Spirit, one hope. How is such unity possible when there are so many differences among people?

MAKING THE DIFFERENCE (COMMUNITY)

After reading the Making the Difference (Community) section, answer the following questions.

1. Our community is paralyzed by sin. There is more immorality, divorce, drug abuse, and violence than at any time in our nation's history. What can the church do to help bring about the spiritual healing necessary?

2. How can the church "love their neighbor" and "serve in love" those without faith or those who do not know Jesus?

LIVING IN VICTORY (PERSONAL)

After reading the Living in Victory (Personal) section, answer the following questions.

1. Take a few minutes to take stock of your physical and spiritual health. How healthy are you? Are you in need of healing? What kind? Do you have the faith necessary to achieve victory over sin and sickness?

2. Do you believe healing is complete without forgiveness? Why or why not?

3. When was the last time you acted as part of a network of faith? What did you do? How was your act received? How can you convince others to "step up to the plate"?

PRAYER FORUM

Write a prayer or words of inspiration thanking God for helping you to forgive others who have hurt you.

STEPS ON THE WAY TO VICTORY

BASED ON JOSHUA 2:1, 8–16, 22–24

KEY VERSE: *"And as soon as we had heard these things, our hearts did melt, neither did there remain any more courage in any man, because of you: for the LORD your God, he is God in heaven above, and in earth beneath" (Joshua 2:11).*

LESSON FOCUS

It is the intention of God to give us victory, and to aid us in our walk into victory over all the challenges in life that we face. It is God's intention to grant us victory over people and things, which seek to keep us in the wilderness as perpetual wanderers.

As we seek to gain our victory, we must not neglect the necessary mental, physical, and spiritual preparation required for living a victorious life. Are you prepared? Let God help you! Let God take you to a place where you cannot only smell victory but see it—even before it comes to pass.

DO YOU KNOW...?

To prepare for this lesson, study the following words and definitions (all are taken from Chapter 5—"Steps on the Way to Victory").

Canaan—the Promised Land; area where the City of Jericho was located

Jericho—the walled city captured by Joshua; one of the oldest known, continually occupied cities in human history. Its origin goes back to at least 7000 B.C.

reconnaissance mission—a project involving the exploration of an area for military purposes

spies—foot soldiers. Joshua and Moses both sent spies to determine the situation in the land. Moses sent 12 spies; 10 returned with negative reports. Joshua only sent two.

INTRODUCTION (REAL LIFE) DISCUSSION QUESTIONS

After reading the Introduction (Real Life) section, answer the following questions.

1. Should former prostitutes or those who have been in jail for serious crimes be allowed to serve as leaders in the church? Why or why not?

2. If Joshua truly trusted God, why did he send spies into the land of Canaan, especially the city of Jericho? If God tells us that we will have the victory in our lives, should we "send out spies" to survey the situation?

____

____

____

3. All victory belongs to God and He will help prepare us to face the physical, mental, and spiritual challenges that will plague us daily. Given this, are you prepared to claim victory? If not, what can you do to prepare?

____

____

____

A WORD FROM THE LORD

SCRIPTURE SEARCH

Read Joshua 2:1, 8–16, 22–24, and then use the following questions to review the facts from this Scripture passage.

1. Rahab told the two spies that the Canaanites heard about the deliverance Yahweh (Jehovah) had given them to do what (Joshua 2:10)?

____

2. Rahab boldly declared that Yahweh, God of the Hebrews, was what (v. 11)?

____

3. What did Rahab use to let the spies out of her window (v. 15)?

____

4. How long did the spies hide in the mountains before returning to their camp (v. 22)?

____

5. What sort of report did the spies bring back to Joshua (v. 24)?

____

____

6. Read Joshua 2:8–11. Then answer the following questions. Then write down five points stated in a confession by Rahab to help the spies see what God had already done in Jericho.

a. ____

b. ______________________________

c. ______________________________

d. ______________________________

e. ______________________________

7. Explain how Rahab's words signaled a victory for the Israelites.

____

____

8. Only two adults, who left Egypt with Moses, entered the Promised Land. Who were they? See Numbers 14:24 and Deuteronomy 31:7 and write their names below.

____

____

9. Why do you think God kept those two alive?

____

____

10. Read Luke 16:9. Then discuss its relevance in our walk into victory.

____

____

____

____

11. How did going "into the enemy camp" help the spies Joshua sent?

____

____

12. As we move into battle to claim our victory, we need to be careful to understand the things that hinder our walk with the Lord. Read 1 Peter 5:8–9. Discuss whether or not this warning is taken as seriously as it ought to be.

____

____

____

____

MAKING THE DIFFERENCE (COMMUNITY)

After reading the Making the Difference (Community) section, answer the following questions.

1. How might Christians actually "spy out" (examine and understand) today's serious social problems in order to help solve them?

2. Too many churches fail because people carry negative experiences and rehearse details over and over until the whole psyche of the church is pathological and relationships have become demonized. What does a church like this need to do to heal?

LIVING IN VICTORY (PERSONAL)

After reading the Living in Victory (Personal) section, answer the following questions.

1. Is there a place for the "Rahabs" in our society? How would you respond to such a person? Does God sometimes use "bad" people and situations to carry out His good purposes?

2. Read Joshua 1:5. How can you apply this Scripture as you face life's daily challenges?

3. The greatest victory we have is the victory won for us through the life, death, and resurrection of Jesus. Why is that our greatest victory? When was the last time you shared that victory with someone?

PRAYER FORUM

Write a prayer or words of inspiration thanking God for guiding you to victory.

THE VICTORY OF JOSEPH

BASED ON GENESIS 37:3–4, 17–28; 41:14–16, 25–40

KEY VERSE: *"And Pharaoh said unto Joseph, Forasmuch as God hath shewed thee all this, there is none so discreet and wise as thou art" (Genesis 41:39).*

LESSON FOCUS

God's favor is not dependent upon anything but God's goodness. God's favor cannot be earned. God loves us and provides for us because we are His. Even when we face adversities, we are His.

DO YOU KNOW...?

To prepare for this lesson, study the following words and definitions (all are taken from Chapter 6—"The Victory of Joseph").

coat of many colors—ornate tunic (robe)

cupbearer—a high-ranking, trustworthy officer who served wine to the king

Egypt—located in Northwest Africa, it was one of the earliest civilizations as well as one of the most powerful nations

INTRODUCTION (REAL LIFE) DISCUSSION QUESTIONS

After reading the Introduction (Real Life) section, answer the questions.

1. Describe what problem(s) can be created in a church because of a favored status?

2. Describe what problem(s) can be created in a family because of a favored status?

3. If you have ever received better or special treatment, how did/do you feel? Did you deserve the special favors or turn them down?

4. List some of the reasons why you think people respond negatively/positively to others with favor.

A WORD FROM THE LORD

SCRIPTURE SEARCH

Read Genesis 37:3–4, 17–28; 41:14–16, 25–40, and then use the following questions to review the facts from this Scripture passage.

1. Why did Joseph's brothers hate him (Genesis 37:4)?

2. What did Joseph's brothers' anger lead them to do (vv. 18, 27–28)?

3. Did Joseph promise a positive dream interpretation to Pharaoh (41:16)?

4. What was the basic meaning of Pharaoh's dream (v. 25)?

5. What did Joseph suggest that Pharaoh do to prepare for what was about to happen (v. 34)?

6. What are some of the adversities that Joseph faced?

a. Genesis 37:4

b. verse 18

c. verse 24

d. verse 28

Remaining Faithful During Adversity

1. Joseph's story is one of perseverance. He inherited the ability to forgive and overcome the hurt of betrayal and the faith in God to restore and redeem. What do you believe kept Joseph from becoming bitter or even angry with God over his years of adversity? Discuss how you can apply this quality to your own life.

____

____

____

2. The following Scriptures speak on faith. Fill in the blanks with the correct words. Try to fill in the blanks before looking up the Scripture.

a. "Jesus said unto him, If thou canst ______________, all things are __________________ to him that believeth" (Mark 9:23).

b. "Even so________________, if hath not __________, is dead, being alone" (James 2:17).

c. "And the ______________ of faith shall save the sick, and the Lord ____________ _____________ him up; and if he have ________________ sins, they shall be forgiven him" (James 5:15).

d. "My brethren, count it all __________ when ye fall into divers ___________________; Knowing this, that the trying of your faith ____________ ______________" (James 1:2–3).

e. "Wherein ye greatly rejoice, though now for a season, if need be, ye are in ___________________ through manifold temptations: That the _____________ of your faith, being much more precious than of _______________ that perisheth, though it be tried with fire, might be found unto _____________ and _____________ and glory at the appearing of Jesus Christ" (1 Peter 1:6–7).

Ultimate Triumph over Adversity

1. Select a Scripture from Genesis 37, 40, or 41 that talks about living in adversity. Discuss how remembering that Scripture, even when facing adversity, will help you.

____

____

____

2. Read Genesis 41:14–16, 25–40.

a. Why do you think God had Pharaoh and Joseph connect through dreams?

____

____

b. Can you think of a time the Lord's hand moved in your own life? Explain.

MAKING THE DIFFERENCE (COMMUNITY)

Answer the following questions after reading the Making the Difference (Community) section.

1. How should a church, as a whole, face adversity?

2. Can Christian families be dysfunctional? If yes, how?

3. What is the responsibility of parents, children, grandparents, and other relatives in maintaining family harmony and unity?

4. Is the church charged with the responsibility to families in its community? Why or why not? Support your answers with Scripture.

LIVING IN VICTORY (PERSONAL)

After reading the Living in Victory (Personal) section, answer the following questions.

1. Why did God's providence for Joseph include so much suffering? What did you learn from his suffering?

2. How do the gracious acts of God toward us form the foundation for our move to victory?

3. How did God preserve both Joseph's life and his spirit, and what did you learn from Joseph's experience that can be applied to your life?

4. Joseph's fine qualities were apparent in both bad and good times. Explain what those qualities were. Also explain why you believe this should hold true for all people.

PRAYER FORUM

Write a prayer or words of inspiration that are related to the chapter's theme.

VICTORY OVER BOUNDARIES

BASED ON MATTHEW 8:5–13

KEY VERSE: *"And Jesus said unto the centurion, Go thy way; and as thou hast believed, so be it done unto thee. And his servant was healed in the selfsame hour" (Matthew 8:13).*

LESSON FOCUS

Boundaries are walls of segregation, unspoken lines we don't want to cross, or fences we've built around our hearts. Sometimes boundaries are imposed on us by other people who are different than we are, people who feel they are superior to others and don't want to mix with others. Sometimes we impose our own boundaries, like the barrier that sin creates between humans and God.

Thanks be to God, Jesus has broken boundaries. From the barrier that separates us from our Holy God to gender, nationality, and other boundaries, Jesus has erased the line and made it possible for us to commune with our Lord and each other.

DO YOU KNOW. . . ?

To prepare for this lesson, study the following words and definitions (all are taken from Chapter 7—"Victory Over Boundaries").

the boundaries of times—the Israelites (Jews) were God's chosen people and thought everyone else was beneath them: Jews did not associate with Gentiles who were considered unclean; entering a Gentile's home would make a Jew ceremoniously unclean

centurion—a commander of 100 soldiers in the Roman army

Gentiles—non-Jewish people or tribes

INTRODUCTION (REAL LIFE) DISCUSSION QUESTIONS

Answer reading the Introduction (Real Life) section, answer the following questions.

1. In what way is Sunday representative of the division between and among groups of people?

____

____

____

2. Are the barriers that separate races, genders, and socioeconomic classes natural or learned? Why?

3. What experiences might a person have that reveal there are barriers in his or her life?

A WORD FROM THE LORD

SCRIPTURE SEARCH

Read Matthew 8:5–13, and then use the following questions to review the facts from this Scripture passage.

1. Who approached Jesus when He entered Capernaum (Matthew 8:5)?

2. What did the man want from Jesus (v. 6)?

3. Where was the sick man (v. 6)?

4. What did Jesus say when the centurion told Him the servant was sick (v. 7)?

5. What was the centurion's response to Jesus' answer (vv. 8–9)?

6. What was Jesus' response to the centurion's faith (vv. 10–13)?

____

____

7. What did Jesus say would happen to many people from the east and west (v. 11)?

____

____

____

God Is Holy

Our God is a Holy God; recognizing His holiness should make us understand why sin creates a barrier between us. Use a concordance to find each Scripture. Then write who is speaking and why.

1. "There is none holy as the LORD: for there is none beside thee: neither is there any rock like our God."

   Scripture: ______________________________

   Who is speaking? ______________________________

   Why? ______________________________

2. "The LORD is righteous in all his ways, and holy in all his works."

   Scripture: ______________________________

   Who is speaking? ______________________________

   Why? ______________________________

3. "Who shall not fear thee, O Lord, and glorify thy name? for thou only art holy: for all nations shall come and worship before thee; for thy judgments are made manifest."

   Scripture: ______________________________

   Who is speaking? ______________________________

   Why? ______________________________

4. "And he said, Draw not nigh hither: put off thy shoes from off thy feet, for the place whereon thou standest is holy ground."

   Scripture: ______________________________

   Who is speaking? ______________________________

   Why? ______________________________

Sin Separates Us from Our Holy God

1. Use the Scriptures to find out what God says about sin and what it does to our relationship with our Holy God. Fill in the blanks.

a. "Behold, all souls are ________; as the soul of the father, so also the soul of the son is mine: the soul that ___________, it shall die" (Ezekiel 18:4).

b. "For the wages of _______ is _______; but the gift of God is _________ life through Jesus Christ our Lord" (Romans 6:23).

c. "For if we ______ willfully after that we have received the knowledge of the _______, there remaineth no more sacrifice for sins" (Hebrews 10:26).

d. "And he that doubteth is damned if he eat, because he eateth not of ________: for whatsoever is not of faith is _______" (Romans 14:23).

e. "If we say we have no _______, we deceive ___________, and the truth is not in us" (1 John 1:8).

f. "If we confess our _______, he is faithful and just to forgive us our sins, and to _______ us from all unrighteousness" (1 John 1:9).

g. "And now they ________ more and ________, and have made them molten images of their silver, and idols according to their own understanding, all of it the work of the craftsmen: they say of them, Let the men that sacrifice kiss the calves" (Hosea 13:2).

2. Define the sins listed in Galatians 5:19–21 and give modern-day examples. (The examples will vary.)

a. adultery ____

b. fornication ____

c. uncleanness ____

d. lasciviousness ____

e. idolatry ____

f. witchcraft ____

g. hatred ____

h. variance ____

i. emulations ____

j. wrath ____

k. strife ____

l. seditions ____

m. heresies ____

n. envyings ____

o. murders ____

p. drunkenness ____

q. revellings ____

Jesus Broke the Barrier Between God and Man

God's design was for His people to live eternally and in harmony with our Maker. However, we let God down and sin crept onto the scene. Sin separates us from God, but He made a way for us to live with Him eternally through the sin offering of Jesus.

Trace the history of mankind's tumultuous relationship with God by numbering the following incidents in order of occurrence. Then find the Scripture references to describe each event.

_____ God became extremely angry with the sins of the people so He sent a flood. _____________

_____ God created the beautiful Garden of Eden for Adam to dwell in. ________________

_____ The 12 tribes of Israel were born through Jacob and Leah, Rachel, Zilphah, Bilhah. ________________

_____ Satan persuaded Eve to eat of the Tree of Knowledge of Good and Evil, and she persuaded Adam to eat, too. ___________________________

_____ God cursed the serpent, Adam, and Eve for their sin. ________________________

_____ Jesus conquered death. ____________________________

_____ God promised to tear apart the united kingdom of Israel because of Solomon's insistence on worshiping idols. _____________________

_____ Cain was marked by God for killing his brother, Abel. _____________________

_____ God instructed Adam to eat from all of the trees in the garden except the Tree of Knowledge of Good and Evil. _________________________

_____ Eve was created from Adam's rib. ________________________

_____ As the people built a tower to get to heaven, God mixed the people's languages so they could not understand each other. ___________________________

_____ God planted the Tree of Knowledge of Good and Evil in the garden. ______________________

_____ Jesus died and the curtain in the temple was torn. ________________________

_____ A famine brought the Children of Israel to Egypt. ___________________________

_____ God sent Moses to deliver His people. ___________________________

_____ The Israelites rejected God and asked for a king. _____________________________

_____ The Messiah was born. ____________________________

_____ God promised to bless Abram. ____________________________

_____ The Pharach of Egypt rejected the Israelites and made them slaves. _____________________

Jesus Breaks Barriers on Earth

Discuss the barriers set up in the following situations, and write what Jesus said to the people to break the barriers.

1. the Samaritan woman at the well (John 4:13–14)

____

____

____

2. the Gentile mother (Mark 7:29)

____

____

____

3. the woman caught in adultery (John 8:11)

4. the man with a crippled hand (Mark 3:1–5)

The following Scriptures tell us what God says about barriers. Match the Scripture with the barrier.

James 2:2–9	Show compassion toward prisoners.
Hebrews 13:3	Teach all nations.
Matthew 28:19	Everyone, regardless of nationality, gender, or position is
John 3:16	the same in Christ.
Galatians 3:28	Do not show favoritism for the rich and well-dressed.
	Whoever believes in God's Son shall have everlasting life.

MAKING THE DIFFERENCE (COMMUNITY)

After reading the Making the Difference (Community) section, answer the following questions.

1. What barriers exist within your church community among different races, genders, or socioeconomic groups?

2. What programs can be instituted to help break down barriers?

3. Who is suffering in your community? What can be done to help them and how?

LIVING IN VICTORY (PERSONAL)

After reading the Living in Victory (Personal) section, answer the following questions.

1. What sins separate you from God? Confess your sins and be cleansed.

2. What separates you from others who are of a different race, gender, socioeconomic group, etc.?

3. How can you break those barriers?

PRAYER FORUM

Write a prayer asking God's help in removing the barriers that keep you from full fellowship with God, family, or others. Make a commitment to rectify the issues that separate you and to ask God's help in restoring relationships.

EQUIPPED FOR VICTORY

BASED ON MATTHEW 4:1–11

KEY VERSE: *"Then saith Jesus unto him, Get thee hence, Satan: for it is written, Thou shalt worship the Lord thy god, and him only shalt thou serve" (Matthew 4:10).*

LESSON FOCUS

In order to follow in step with the Master, we must be guided by the Word of God. Learning, understanding, and applying God's Word in our lives is essential for us to grow in our spiritual maturity and to share the Word of God with others.

DO YOU KNOW...?

To prepare for this lesson, study the following words and definitions (all are taken from Chapter 8—"Equipped for Victory").

logos—word or expression

temptation—enticement; a test of character

wilderness—a barren region

INTRODUCTION (REAL LIFE) DISCUSSION QUESTIONS

Answer the questions after reading the Introduction (Real Life) section.

1. In order to understand God's Word, do you think the Bible and additional resources should be read and studied?

____

____

____

2. Name the publications you think Andina and Shanab used before they started reading the Bible. What resources do you use in church and/or at home to help you better understand the Bible?

____

____

3. Share different ways that we can enhance our own personal Bible study time and how we can encourage others to read and apply the Word to their lives personally and collectively as Andina and Shanab learned to do. How important was the pastor in the Bible study?

A WORD FROM THE LORD

SCRIPTURE SEARCH

Read Matthew 4:1–11, and then use the following questions to review the facts from this Scripture passage.

1. Describe what you think the wilderness looked like.

2. Why did Satan try to tempt Jesus?

3. Why does Jesus respond to Satan by quoting Scriptures?

4. How do you think the angels "ministered" to Jesus?

5. “Inspired” comes from the Greek word meaning “God-breathed.” What does 2 Timothy 3:16 say about the Scriptures? Check the correct answer.

____ Some of the Bible is inspired by God

____ All of the Bible is inspired by God.

____ Only the New Testament is inspired by God.

____ Only the parts of the Bible that speak to you are inspired by God.

6. Do you think Satan knew he would lose in a challenge against Jesus? If so, why would he start a battle with Jesus? If not, why do you think he thought he would win?

____

____

____

7. Describe the relationship of the Word of God to spiritual truth (Numbers 23:19; Psalm 119:151–152; John 17:17).

____

____

____

What Is the Word?

An analogy is comparing two pairs of something that have the same relationship. Look up the verses below and use them to answer the questions that follow.

1. Jeremiah 5:14 and 23:29

a. What is God’s Word compared with?

____

____

____

b. What are the functions of these objects?

____

____

____

c. What does this analogy teach about the Word of God (see also Isaiah 55:11)?

____

2. Matthew 4:4 and 1 Peter 2:2

a. What is God's Word compared with?

b. What are the functions of these objects?

c. What does this analogy teach about the Word of God?

3. Luke 8:11 and 1 Peter 1:23

a. What is God's Word compared with?

b. What is the function of this object?

c. What does this analogy teach about the Word of God?

4. Ephesians 5:26

a. What is God's Word compared with?

b. What is the function of this object?

c. What does this analogy teach about the Word of God?

The Word as Written

1. How was the written Word of God given to us (2 Peter 1:20–21)?

2. How long will the Word of God last (Isaiah 40:8; Matthew 24:34–35; Luke 21:33; 1 Peter 1:24–25)?

3. Who is the central character of the written Word of God (Luke 24:27, 44; John 5:39, 46; 20:31)?

MAKING THE DIFFERENCE (COMMUNITY)

After reading the Making the Difference (Community) section, answer the following questions.

1. How can the members of the congregation be encouraged to witness to others and invite them to church to hear the Word of God?

2. It has been said that 20% of the congregation usually does 80% of the work. Does this saying seem true for your church? How can the members be encouraged to become doers of the Word?

LIVING IN VICTORY (PERSONAL)

After reading the Living in Victory (Personal) section, answer the following questions.

1. Consider the following questions in light of Jesus' example in Matthew 4:1–11.

a. What kinds of hard times have you faced lately?

b. How have you responded to them?

c. Have you ever felt that as a Christian you should be protected from temptations and trials?

d. Read 1 Corinthians 10:13. Consider how you can adjust your perspective according to the Word of God in the midst of tough times.

2. Decide to effectively apply the Word of God. List some areas in your life where you are facing challenges or difficulty. Use a topical Bible to find the commandments, instructions, or promises in God's Word that address these areas. (Where there are no specific Scriptures, find out what scriptural principles apply.) Write the Scriptures on a card or piece of paper so that you can carry them with you. Memorize and meditate on these Scriptures so you can become equipped to walk in victory.

PRAYER FORUM

Write a prayer or words of inspiration related to the chapter's theme.

PREPARATION FOR ULTIMATE VICTORY

BASED ON MATTHEW 24:45–25:13

KEY VERSES: *"Who then is a faithful and wise servant, whom his lord hath made ruler over his household, to give them meat in due season? Blessed is that servant, whom his lord when he cometh shall find so doing" (Matthew 24:45–46).*

LESSON FOCUS

God is calling for believers to be victorious in our everyday Christian living. He is calling for us to be watchful and faithful servants, who are wise and diligent in helping Him to build His kingdom, which will consist of everyone who has believed on the Lord Jesus Christ as their Personal Saviour (John 3:16). Therefore, we need to be vigilant. This need for vigilance is also affirmed in Jesus' statement: "Watch therefore, for ye know neither the day nor the hour wherein the Son of man cometh" (Matthew 25:13). When we follow the blueprint that is found in God's holy, inerrant Word, these challenges are not impossibilities.

DO YOU KNOW. . . ?

To prepare for this lesson, study the following words and definitions (all are taken from Chapter 9—"Preparation for Ultimate Victory").

grace—unearned, unmerited favor

Holy Writ—God's Word, the Bible

parable—a short narrative story told using earthly analogies to illustrate a spiritual truth

procrastination—to put off, to delay

slothful—apathetic, lazy, inactive

victory—conquest, success, win

vigilance—alertness, caution, watchfulness

INTRODUCTION (REAL LIFE) DISCUSSION QUESTIONS

After reading the Introduction (Real Life) section, answer the following questions.

1. How can procrastination cause harm in a person's life?

____

2. How can one gain victory over procrastination?

____

____

____

A WORD FROM THE LORD

SCRIPTURE SEARCH

Read Matthew 24:51–25:13, and then use the following questions to review the facts from this Scripture passage.

What does it mean to be faithful? God is faithful, and faithfulness reveals our likeness to our God. Faithfulness demands that we are worthy of divine trust. Review the selected list from the cloud of faithful witnesses in Hebrews 11.

Now find out where their faithful stories appear in the Bible, read their accounts, and determine how their faithfulness reveals the likeness of God.

a. Enoch

____

____

b. Rahab

____

____

c. Gideon

____

____

d. Jephthah

____

____

Victory for the Prepared

1. In the parable of the 10 virgins, it is important to remember that all of the bridesmaids grew tired of waiting and went to sleep. The difference, however, was that five of the bridesmaids prepared for Christ's coming before going to bed. How are we to be like the five wise virgins? How are we to prepare before resting, especially when we've grown weary and tired? Some of the answers are in the following Scriptures. Find them and the missing words.

a. "He giveth ____________________ to the _______________; and to them that have no _________________ he ____________________ ______________________. Even the youths shall _______________ and be

_____________________ and the young men shall utterly _________________: But they that ______________ upon the LORD shall ______________ their ____________________; they shall __________________ up with wings as eagles; they shall run, and not be ______________________; and they shall walk, and not ______________" (Isaiah 40:29–31).

b. "For ______________ is not unrighteous to _______________ your ________________ and ____________________ of love, which ye have shewed toward his _________________, in that ye have ______________________________ to the saints, and do ________________. And we desire that every one of you shew the same ______________________ to the full assurance of hope unto the end: That ye be not ___________________, but followers of them who through _______________ and __________________ inherit the promises" (Hebrews 6:10–12).

c. "Come unto me, all ye that __________________ and are heavy ________________, and I will give you ____________. Take my _______________ upon you, and learn of me; for I am _______________ and _____________ in heart: and ye shall find ____________ unto your souls. For my ______________ is ____________, and my ____________________ is ________________" (Matthew 11:28–30).

d. "But the end of all things is at ______________: be ye therefore _____________, and ________________ unto ____________________" (1 Peter 4:7).

e. "Be __________________, be ______________________; because your adversary the _______________, as a roaring lion, walketh about, seeking whom he may ________________: Whom resist __________________ in the ____________, knowing that the same _________________ are accomplished in your brethren that are in the world. But the ___________ of all ______________, who hath called us unto his eternal glory by ______________ ___________________, after that ye have ______________________ a ____________________, make you ____________________, stablish, _________________, _________________ you" (1 Peter 5:8–10).

f. " ____________________ ye, stand _______________ in the _________________, quit you like men, be ______________________" (1 Corinthians 16:13).

The Victorious Attitude and Heart

If we intend to have victory, we must cultivate a certain kind of atmosphere in our hearts. God will reach out to us when we seek him with our hearts.

a. Read Psalm 42:1–2. Imagine you are a hart or deer desiring water. Write down the images that you see as you think of yourself as a deer longing for water. Compare them to how a Christian should long for God.

b. Read Luke 12:31–34. Discuss different places we have set up treasures. How do those places determine where our hearts are? How can we set up treasures in heaven?

Victory through the Holy Spirit

As he/she seeks to remain in the center of God's divine will, the faithful servant is convinced of the power of God to sustain him/her in all circumstances that may arise. Read the following Scriptures and write how they can help Christians rely on God's power. Which one relates to you the most?

a. Matthew 28:18–20

b. Acts 6:8

c. Acts 8:4–8

d. Ephesians 1:19–20

e. Luke 24:46–49

MAKING THE DIFFERENCE (COMMUNITY)

After reading the Making the Difference (Community) section, answer the following questions.

1. How can your church impart to others the importance that knowledge of Christ's return is not sufficient for entrance into His eternal reign? How can you inform others that the knowledge must be accompanied by preparation?

2. Jesus emphasizes the importance of praying for the power of the Holy Spirit. How much time in your church is spent "tarrying" (waiting) and praying for power for your congregation? Compare the amount of prayer time to the time given to other activities.

3. How can your church encourage members to move beyond the mediocre and take hold of the power God provides?

LIVING IN VICTORY (PERSONAL)

After reading the Living in Victory (Personal) section, answer the following questions.

1. How are you preparing for the return of Christ?

2. Review your actions, thoughts, and conversations from this week. Were you more like the faithful servant or the evil servant? Explain.

3. How are you attending to your call and commitment to serve? What can you do differently to be more obedient to God's will?

4. Read Lamentations 3:22–23. How is God faithful to you? How are you faithful to God? Determine to be faithful to the Great Faithful One (God).

PRAYER FORUM

Write a prayer or words of inspiration on preparation for ultimate victory (the second coming of Jesus).

NOTES

NOTES